JENEVIEVE CHANG is a writer, performer and story developer for stage and screen. Her memoir *The Good Girl of Chinatown* was published by Penguin Random House in 2017 and Jenevieve's playwriting debut, *Yong*, won the 2023 Sydney Theatre Award for Best Production for Children. Jenevieve has also written a number of radio plays for ABC Radio National. Jenevieve was most recently Development Executive at ABC Drama & Comedy, where her credits include *House of Gods* (2023), *White Fever* (2024) and the hit comedy *Austin* (2024). Prior to that, Jenevieve was Development Executive at Screen Australia. As a performer, Jenevieve has worked with Malthouse Theatre, Bell Shakespeare, Griffin Theatre and Monkey Baa Theatre in Australia; and The National Theatre, The Young Vic, Yellow Earth Theatre, Chopped Logic and Fran Barbe Dance in the UK. Between 2008–2011, Jenevieve lived and worked in Shanghai where she was one of the founding members of China's first Vaudeville, Variety and Burlesque clubs. Jenevieve is currently BA Discipline Lead for Screenwriting at the Australian Film, Television and Radio School.

# YONG

ADAPTED FOR THE STAGE
BY JENEVIEVE CHANG

BASED ON THE BOOK
BY JANEEN BRIAN

**CURRENCY PRESS**
The performing arts publisher

CURRENCY PLAYS

First published in 2025
by Currency Press Pty Ltd,
Gadigal Land, Suite 310, 46–56 Kippax Street, Surry Hills, NSW 2010, Australia
enquiries@currency.com.au
www.currency.com.au

Copyright: © Jenevieve Chang, 2025; based on the original novel *Yong* © 2016, Janeen Brian.

The moral rights of the authors have been asserted.

COPYING FOR EDUCATIONAL PURPOSES

The Australian *Copyright Act 1968* [Act] allows a maximum of one chapter or 10% of this book, whichever is the greater, to be copied by any educational institution for its educational purposes provided that that educational institution [or the body that administers it] has given a remuneration notice to Copyright Agency [CA] under the Act.

For details of the CA licence for educational institutions contact CA, 12 / 66 Goulburn Street, Sydney, NSW, 2000; tel: within Australia 1800 066 844 toll free; outside Australia 61 2 9394 7600; fax: 61 2 9394 7601; email: memberservices@copyright.com.au

COPYING FOR OTHER PURPOSES

Except as permitted under the Act, for example a fair dealing for the purposes of study, research, criticism or review, no part of this book may be reproduced, stored in a retrieval system, or transmitted in any form or by any means without prior written permission. All enquiries should be made to the publisher at the address above.

No part of this book may be used or reproduced in any manner for the purpose of training artificial intelligence technologies or systems without the express written permission of the author and the publisher.

Any performance or public reading of *Yong* is forbidden unless a licence has been received from the author or the author's agent. The purchase of this book in no way gives the purchaser the right to perform the play in public, whether by means of a staged production or a reading. All applications for public performance should be addressed to the author c / — Zeitgeist Agency, query_sydney@zeitgeistagency.com.

Currency Press has made every reasonable effort to identify, and gain the permission of, the artists who appear in the photographs that illustrate this play.

Typeset by Brighton Gray for Currency Press.
Cover design by Kim Siew for Currency Press.

Currency Press acknowledges the Traditional Owners of the Country on which we live and work. We pay our respects to all Aboriginal and Torres Strait Islander Elders, past and present.

# Contents

*Writer's Note*   *xiii*

YONG   1

*Wern Mak as Yong in Monkey Baa's production of YONG 2022 (Photo: Tiffany Garvie)*

# Writer's Note

When Monkey Baa first approached me to adapt Janeen Brian's *Yong: The Journey of An Unworthy Son*, I was a new mother, barely sleeping, utterly in love with my baby boy—and deeply overwhelmed. It was 2020, the world was in lockdown, and the future felt precarious. I was riddled with questions about how to raise a child in a world that felt like it was falling apart. How do you find your footing in a time of such uncertainty? How do you pass on courage when you're not sure you possess it yourself?

As if in answer, *Yong* came into my life. In witnessing the rising tide of anti-Chinese sentiment—here in Australia and around the world—the idea of telling this story felt vital. A boy: Chinese, brave, vulnerable. His journey from southern China to the goldfields of nineteenth-century Australia felt both timely and timeless. It became my act of resistance: a story about humanity, not headlines. History, not hate.

But *Yong* is not just a migration story. It's the story of a boy mourning his mother and leaving his homeland, trying desperately to live up to the weight of his father's expectations. It's about learning that love doesn't always look like what we expect it to. It's about honouring where you come from while finding the courage to become who you can be.

As someone who migrated to Australia as a child, I recognised so much of myself in Yong—his yearning, his confusion, his longing to be understood. Writing this play became a letter to my son. A lighthouse, I hope, for when life feels impossibly dark and difficult to navigate. Because we all face moments when we feel small and unsure—when we're trying to find our place, our voice, our way.

One of the key creative challenges in adapting the novel was considering how to bring a world of characters to life through just one performer. What began as a constraint became a revelation—an invitation to embrace theatricality in its purest form. I also wanted to reflect the nuance of language—the intimate, familial tension of things that go unsaid between father and son, contrasted with the jarring awkwardness of speaking outside their mother tongue.

In finding Yong's voice, I found myself drawn to the contemporary. Playing with anachronism helped make him feel alive—like someone who could walk into a room today and still be relevant—because, ultimately, Yong is not a relic of the past. He is every young person navigating grief, identity, duty and hope. He is every child trying to be seen.

I am deeply grateful to Monkey Baa's Artistic Director Eva Di Cesare, whose belief in the power of stories for young people is unwavering, and to company co-founder Sandie Eldridge, who brainstormed and walked the early steps of this journey with me.

Thank you to Kevin du Preez, Emma Khamis, Alexander Andrews, and the whole Monkey Baa family for your fierce commitment to young minds and big ideas.

We were incredibly fortunate to have Darren Yap as both director and dramaturg. Darren brought not only his extraordinary talent but also his big, generous heart. His commitment to the work—both as an artist and as a descendant of those early Chinese pioneers in search of gold—unlocked new possibilities and instilled a confidence in my practice that continues to sustain.

Speaking of good fortune, I had the dexterous talents of Wern Mak in those early days to test and refine all the ways I could fit the story of all those characters into one actor's body. Then, the wonderful George Zhao stepped into Yong's shoes and interrogated every line and every word for sense, meaning, clarity and accuracy.

Production designer James Browne made the whole world of *Yong* look glorious, and Max Lambert composed a score that opened up a nineteenth-century world through a twenty-first-century lens.

*Yong* premiered at Ballarat Civic Hall in August 2022. In the lead-up, the local Chinese-Australian community, led by Charles Zhang, recorded a lullaby my own mother used to sing, which now threads through the show as a gentle act of remembrance. It was a moment where personal memory met collective history, and I was reminded once again of why we make theatre: to heal, to imagine, to connect.

Finally, I am indebted to Richard Frankland, whose literary craft and cultural knowledge of Gunditjmara country and language is expressed in Scene Fourteen.

Always was, always will be.

*Jenevieve Chang*

*Wern Mak as Yong in Monkey Baa's production of* Yong *2022 (Photo: Tiffany Garvie)*

*Yong* was produced by Monkey Baa Theatre Company in collaboration with the Chinese community and broader community of Ballarat, in partnership with Her Majesty's Theatre Ballarat and Capitol Theatre Bendigo. *Yong* was first performed at Ballarat Civic Hall, Wadawurrung Country, on 27 August 2022, with the following cast and creatives:

        YONG                             Wern Mak

Director, Darren Yap
Production Designer, James Browne
Composer, Max Lambert
Lighting Designer, Ben Brockman
Movement Director, Angie Diaz
Sound Designer, Zac Saric
Adaptation Consultant, Sandra Eldridge
Chinese Consultant, Charles Zhang
Illustration, Kim Siew
First Nations Consultant and Writer of First Nations Scene, Richard Frankland

*Wern Mak as Yong in Monkey Baa's production of YONG 2022 (Photo: Tiffany Garvie)*

**CHARACTERS**

YONG
NING
CHUNG
SAILOR, voiceover
PASSENGERS, voiceover
BOAT OWNER, voiceover
GRANDMA, voiceover
ENGLISH LADY, voiceover
FOREIGN MAN 1, voiceover
FOREIGN MAN 2, voiceover
FENG
GEORGE
MUTT THE DOG, heard not seen

**NOTE**

All onstage characters are played by one actor.

## NOTE ON LANGUAGE/ACCENTS

The play is set in a Chinese storyworld and performed in English. The only time English might sound 'foreign' in the voice of our characters is when speaking cross-culturally to a character for whom English is their first language.

In the 2023 production, some of Grandma's voiceover lines were pre-recorded in Mandarin. The pinyin transliterations of these lines are included in this text. While Cantonese is commonly spoken in Guangdong province, Mandarin was selected as the dialect for Yong's inaugural production. Future production teams are welcome to choose the Chinese dialect that best suits their interpretation of Yong's storyworld and characters.

## PRELUDE

YONG, *a nineteenth-century teenaged boy, appears onstage with a model ship. Placing it on water, the ship teeters.*

*A memory is triggered.*

## SCENE ONE

*Off the coast of South Australia, 1857.*
*Thunder cracks, wind howls, rain falls. The waves crash against the creaky ship.*
YONG *vomits violently over the deck.*

YONG: Pickled vegetables and rice gruel.
    Yuck.
    Awful going down, disgusting coming up.
    Better than nothing, I s'pose.
    Better than the beetles Grandma crushed back in the village.
    When we had nothing else to eat.

*Crash of crockery being smashed with the heaving of the ship.*

YONG *looks up at the sky, at the moon.*

Three full moons since I last saw Grandma.
    And my brothers, and baby sister.
    Sometimes it feels like we've travelled so far from our village
That we'll soon drop off the edge of the world.
    Father says [*clearing his throat*] 'By my estimation, we should arrive any day now.'
    That's Father for you, always sounding like he knows what he's talking about.
    I guess that's why they made him Headman.

YONG *suddenly pulls himself upright.*

Father!
    He's coming at me with a face more thunderous than the storm in the sky,

And straight away I know something isn't right.

*A shudder as the ship heaves to one side. A beam breaks.*

*Lightning streaks through the sky and morphs into strobe.*

*As* YONG *struggles to regain his balance, he reaches for the broken beam.*

FLASHFORWARD BEGINS.

*The pounding of the heart, the screech of anxiety in* YONG*'s head.*

*The beam becomes a tree branch as* YONG *holds it up to strike. A dog barks. A rifle cocks.* YONG *brings down the branch with a distorted scream and collapses.*

FLASHFORWARD ENDS.

NING: Yong! Yong! Are you alright?
YONG: Father, I … I'm alright. I just …
    But seeing as I'm not dead, he's already moved on to the next thing. Gathering boxes, gathering men.
    Everyone's moving at once.
    And I can see I'm not the only one that's sick.
    Mr Feng is practically hanging off the ship, he's retching so hard.
    Father stops to give him a drink,
    Even though all I got was a 'Glad you're not dead!'

YONG *goes to* NING.

[*Tapping him on the shoulder*] Father? What's happen—
NING: Ssh. Not now, Yong! Can't you see I'm busy?
YONG: And suddenly I notice a very tall man staring down at me,
    Unblinking, with only one eye.
    The other eye socket is empty, except for a film of skin.
    Mr Feng's saying something about him being a cousin,
    That he's had bad luck on the journey,
    That all the other men in his village disappeared …
    But I'm not really paying attention because I can't stop wondering
    What happened to this man's other eye?
NING: You are welcome to join us on our journey, Mr Chung.
CHUNG: Thank you, Headman Ning. I have heard great things about you. That you learnt English from the foreigners when you worked on the British ships in Canton.

NING: This is my son, Yong.
   Only thirteen,
   He's still a boy.
YONG: I want to ask Father: 'What's that supposed to mean?'
   But instead, I bow. Obediently.
   Nice to m—

   *The ship gives a great moan and drops with a thud.*

   [*Picking himself up from the floor*] No time for politeness. Hundreds pour out from below deck.
   Sailors toss goods overboard.
   Everywhere I look there seems to be a tangle of men with a tangle of poles, baskets and spades.
   Father?! Father?! Where are you?
   Father!
NING: [*out of breath, stooping to* YONG*'s eye level*] Yong! Stay close.
   And don't forget your promise.
YONG: Of course. The Promise.

   *Chinese voices cry out.*

   Boats!
   They must be coming for us!

   YONG *gets heaved forward.*

NING: [*in English*] What is happening? I would like to talk to the captain, please.
SAILOR: [*voiceover*] You can't talk to the captain; he died a week ago. Get back, the lot of you!

   *The ship creaks.*

   We're beached in Guichen Bay.
NING: No, that not right. We pay tax money so we land Port Phillip Bay. In Victoria. Close to goldfields.
SAILOR: [*voiceover; mimicking*] 'No, that not right!' We were never even sailing to Port Phillip Bay. You got legs, you walk. You walk to the goldfields from South Australia.

   *Chaos and confusion, shouts and cries in Chinese as waves pummel the sides of the ship.*

YONG's *arms struggle with the weight of everything he's brought from China.*

PASSENGER 1: [*voiceover*] Move, boy!

PASSENGER 2: [*voiceover*] Hurry: get out of the way!

YONG *gets pushed over, but a hand catches him.*

YONG: It's the one-eyed stranger. Mr Chung!

CHUNG: Just take one basket. I can help carry the rest of your things.

YONG *reaches for a basket and checks what's inside.*

YONG: Thank you, Mr Chung. I'll take this basket. It's the most important one.

Then I scrabble over the railing, my feet stabbing the air to find the ladder. With every step down, I thank my ancestors that I'm still gripping onto my basket, gripping onto the ladder, gripping onto my life.

Finally, my feet make it to the edge of the rowboat.

*Sound of waves against a rowboat and the creak of oars.*

YONG *clutches his basket against his chest.*

## SCENE TWO

*The bright, harsh glare of the Australian sun.*

*The alien shriek of seagulls, waves on the shore.*

BOAT OWNER: [*voiceover*] All out! Come on. Out ya get. Out!

*A cacophony of sounds as people disembark.*

YONG *steps onto the shoreline.*

*English voices get closer and louder.*

YONG: I've never heard so much English all at once.

The foreigners look so strange with their bright clothes, pink faces and hairy chins.

*Screech of a seagull.*

YONG: [*looking around*] The air makes me thirsty just from breathing.

The light of the sun hurts my skin.

It's so different from home,

With its mists and rain and breeze.

FENG: How far are the goldfields?
NING: Three or four hundred miles. In the foreigners' measurements.
YONG: What's that in our measurement, Father?
NING: A mile is about three *li*.

*Sounds of disbelief and consternation from the villagers.*

YONG: [*shocked*] Is he serious?
We won't get home for months and months!
I can see Grandma watching the seasons come and go, wondering if we're okay. I can see her scraping around for food, trying to feed my brothers and sister. And I can see her brave smile as she said goodbye to us, telling me she would see me soon.
How will we get there, Father?
NING: We will walk. As we have always walked.

*Pause.*

Are you alright, Yong?
YONG: Of course I'm not alright!
Judging from the pale look on everyone else's faces, no-one else is alright either.
But I swallow my feelings.
'I guess I'm just … I'm just hungry. When can we eat?'
NING: Go look for seaweed along the shore.

*Sounds of the shore.*

YONG *bends down, collecting seaweed to put in his cloth bag.*

YONG: [*tasting some*] Salty.

*Screech of a seagull.*

What do they call you, little white seabird with legs of red?
Red's the colour of good luck where I'm from.

YONG *imitates the bird strutting and pecking. With a screech, the seagull flies off as* YONG *watches it disappear over the horizon.*

I wish I could fly off as well, little bird.

*FLASHBACK BEGINS: Rural village, Guangdong.*

*The light changes.*

*Sound of crickets.*

YONG *squats on the earthen floor, playing with his pet cricket.*
[*Whispering*] This famine will end soon. I promise I'll keep you safe, little cricket. I'll keep you safe. No-one will eat you while I'm here.
GRANDMA: [*voiceover in Mandarin*] Yōng, zhǔnbèi hǎo. Bàba hěn kuài jiù dào jiā. Tā yǒu zhòngyào de shìqíng yào gàosù nǐ. (*Yong, please get ready. Your father will be back soon. He has something important to tell you.*)
YONG: What is it, Grandma?
GRANDMA: Gold's been found in a land down south called Australia. You must go.
YONG: But how will you manage on your own?
*FLASHBACK ENDS.* YONG *is still squatting.*
ENGLISH LADY: [*screaming out*] That's disgusting. You dirty celestials.

YONG *stands up quickly, looking up towards the cliff face where the voice came from but no-one is there.*

*Transition sound of waves into next scene.*

SCENE THREE

*Image of Union Jack flying on a flagpole.*
*We hear horses, English voices, laughter.*
YONG *is spun around as he is violently yanked by a passer-by.*
FOREIGN MAN 1: [*waving* YONG*'s pigtail*] Fancy that! It's a boy! Ha, ha, ha. I thought only women had long hair.
FOREIGN MAN 2: Go home, Ching Chong!
*The men walk away, laughing.*
YONG *sits, rubbing his head. Looks at audience.*
YONG: You know what I want to say?
'I *want* to go home! I never *asked* to come! I'd rather starve than be here with animals like you!'
*Sounds of horse hooves clip-clopping in the mud.*
[*Whipping around*] Father!
Did you just see what happened?

But all he wants to talk about is the Promise.
'Yes, Father.
I promise not to let the villagers know I understand English.
Yes, I know it's because you can't let the them "lose face".'
*Beat.*
I watch Father as he walks away, past red buildings, past stone buildings, past faces as pale as parchment.
'Losing face' means to cause embarrassment.
The villagers will be embarrassed because *they* can't speak English, but *I* can.
And that would disrupt the order of the universe, according to Confucius.
After all, I'm just a kid.
*The light changes.* YONG *sends a silent prayer to his ancestors.*
Dear Ma,
Remember on my twelfth birthday, you cooked me fried yam?
And you hid that yam from my brothers for a whole week.
And you were expecting my baby sister to arrive any day.
But still you burrowed away that yam for my birthday even though it meant everyone else went hungry.
Please keep Grandma, my brothers and sister safe until I get home.
I promise I'll find gold, then I'll buy our family all the yams in the world.

SCENE FOUR

*Night noises.*

*Flickering of a campfire.*

YONG *uses his foot to sweep the ground clear of pebbles and twigs, and begins to set up bamboo poles.*

NING: No, Yong! We'll put our tent here.

> YONG *drops the bamboo poles, moves to another spot and starts again.*

Yong! I need you to go fetch some firewood.

> YONG *drops his bamboo poles again.*

YONG: Yes, Father! [*Muttering*] 'Yong this, Yong that' ... Sometimes I wonder if Father's mistaken me for a servant, rather than his son.

> YONG *ducks inside hollow logs and weaves through branches as he gathers wood.*

[*Shivering*] Brrrr, it's cold! This is only enough for one fire. I hope it's enough to boil up a pot of rice.

> YONG *ducks behind a tree.*

[*Under his breath*] Mr Feng!

> *Sounds of burrowing, twigs snapping underfoot.*

I've seen those long pipes before, in the dens of Canton.
And that small parcel ... Uh-oh.

> YONG *comes out of his hiding spot, his eyes following* FENG *as he disappears into the distance. Flames of campfire dancing up towards* YONG'*s face, as the actor morphs into* NING.

> *Rustling, and the sound of men struggling with the weight of a body.*

We haven't seen Mr Feng for hours.
And now they're dragging him into the campsite.

NING: Put him in the tent! [*Looking around*] Who knew Feng was smoking opium?

> *Beat.*

I said, who knew Feng was smoking opium? Li, did you know? Mr Chee? If we are to make it to the goldfields, we cannot have a bad snake among us. I am the Headman, and everything must be reported to me. Speak up! Someone must've known. Yong?

*Looks at* YONG, *realising.*

Yong. Speak up, Yong! [*Shaking* YONG] Speak up, I say!

NING's *shaking morphs into* YONG *being shaken.*

YONG: 'I … I just saw Mr Feng with a pipe. That's all.'
Father is furious.
The eyes of the villagers bore into my skin.
I feel myself crumble,
Why am I arguing with Father?
Again.
*FLASHBACK BEGINS.*

But I don't want to go to Australia!

GRANDMA: [*voiceover in Mandarin*] Háizǐ, nǐ yīnggāi tīng nǐ bàba dehuà. (*Yong, you should do as your father asks.*)

YONG: But, Grandma, I want to stay here with you. Who will look after my brothers if I go? Or my baby sister?

NING: You are coming with me to Australia. That's an order.

YONG: But, Father—

NING: ENOUGH!

*FLASHBACK ENDS.*

## SCENE FIVE

*Sound of men snoring, followed by the chirping of birds as day breaks. Dawn.*

YONG *sneaks out of the cramped tent and searches for more wood. Snapping of twigs behind him.*

YONG: [*whipping around*] Mr Feng!
I back away, but not in time.
I feel his stale breath against my face.

FENG: So, you reported me, eh? What are you, your father's spy?

YONG: 'I didn't mean to cause any trouble, Mr Feng. Father asked me a question and … '

NING: Let him go, Feng. Go splash your face with water. You're lucky you didn't fall off a cliff last night.

*YONG is let go unceremoniously by FENG.*

YONG: 'Thank you, Father. I'm sorry if I caused more—'

*NING turns his back and walks off.*

*Sound of sea hitting the shore.*

*Image of a shapeshifting cloud. The shape gradually morphs into a kite which dances across the sky, its trail morphing into the shapes of embroidered blue and silver chrysanthemums.*

*Mother's song plays. We hear YONG's laughter as a child, and the voice of YONG's mother.*

[*Eyes closed, lost in his daydream*] Coming, Ma! Let me fly my kite just one more time …

*A seagull screech, causing YONG's eyes to snap open.*

I know! Ma's sash!
I can tie it around some twigs to make a kite.
And it'd be just like I was home.

## SCENE SIX

*Back at camp.*

*The light changes.*

YONG: Everything is movement.
All the men are busy preparing to set off.
Mr Chung's been ill, but now he's better.
Mr Li is shuffling through maps.
Mr Feng is haggling over pots.
And Mr Chee is patching his shoes.
But there's only one thing on my mind:

*YONG rummages through the goods in his tent, finds his basket and looks inside.*

Packets of rice. Dried fish. Spare tunic …

YONG *turns the basket around and shakes it. Nothing.*

*A low screech as if it's coming from inside* YONG*'s head, increasing in volume.*

CHUNG: Yong, are you okay?

YONG: 'I've lost something, Mr Chung. I have to find it!'

CHUNG: Maybe your father took it? I saw him take some things into town to trade for money.

*A low screech begins again in* YONG*'s head as he digests this information.*

YONG: Father hasn't even mentioned Ma since she died.
It's as if she didn't even exist.
And now he's gone and taken the one thing I have left from her: Her sash.

## SCENE SEVEN

*The light changes.*

*We hear sounds of the wharf.*

YONG: I can't look Father in the eye, but he doesn't even notice.
I could grow an extra nose and still he wouldn't notice.

NING: [*gesturing*] This way!

YONG: All Father cares about is finding a guide to take us to gold.
Is this what being an adult is all about?
Caring more about money than family?

*A dog barking.*

*Actor becomes* GEORGE.

GEORGE: Mutt! Here! Come here! Goldfields? Yes? I'm a guide, innit. Me cart's over there.
Where d'ya wanna go?

*Leans in to listen and laughs.*

Ball-a-lat? Ball-a-lat? You mean Ballarat, don't you?
Three pounds seven shillings, each man.

*Beat.*

Three pounds four shillings, you say? You must be dreaming. Three pounds six shillings. No? Fine then. I'll do you a favour. Final offer's three pounds five shillings. Can't go any lower. [*Shaking his head*] No. Boy's same price. He's tall like a man, innit?
YONG: My chest swells with pride.
I *am* almost as tall as Father!
I like this man with the battered black hat and blue scarf.
And he has a dog.
Then he smiles, and something unmistakable flashes in his mouth.
A gold tooth!
Surely, this is a sign of good fortune.
GEORGE: Deal? Good. You can call me George. We set off first thing in the morning.

## SCENE EIGHT

*Light rainfall and the clip-clop of horse hooves. A dog barking. Equipment being thrown into a cart.*

NING: [*clapping his hands*] Everybody, line up! Hurry up, Yong! No, Feng. Not there. Yong, stand here.
YONG: Father's put me at the head of the line, just behind him!
Mr Feng looks at me as if he's swallowed something sour.
GEORGE: Gee-up!
*Click of the reins.*
YONG: 'The journey of a thousand miles begins with one step' according to Lao Tzu.
One step, and another step, and another.
But the more I move forward, the more I feel like turning back.

YONG *sings Mother's song and gradually we hear the others join him as they continue to walk.*

*Sound of rain getting heavier.*

YONG *quietly recites words in Mandarin, followed by its English translation: Cloud, Moon. Stars. Dog ...*

*He slips and stumbles. A crash.* YONG *scrambles to his feet.*

I'm so sorry, Mr Feng! Here, let me help—

FENG: Get away from me and watch where you're going, boy.

    YONG *stumbles back and resumes walking.*

YONG: The track is full of holes.

    We don't belong, this track and I.

    Back home, I knew the direction of every house and farm and hill and stream.

    But here, I know nothing.

    I can still hear Mr Feng muttering, 'No-one else was allowed to bring their son,

    Why did we get stuck with him?'

    Mr Chung wants to know if I'm okay.

    I say nothing.

    Pain sears through my ankle.

    But I'm not going to show any weakness.

    Not now.

    Not when Father's right there.

    I don't want him to lose face.

    Because of me.

    *Mutts barking.*

GEORGE: Alright you lot, let's stop 'ere for the night. But don't none of you start getting rowdy on me.

YONG: My legs weigh heavy like lead.

    Today was only our first day. I have no idea how far we walked. I'm afraid to ask.

    Mr Feng is on his soapbox again.

FENG: 'Don't you know the clouds are different in Australia? That's why it rains here in Autumn!'

YONG: But I'm thinking about what Mr Feng said earlier …

    Is it true no-one else from the village was allowed to bring their son?

    Mr Feng's son is a year older than me, a bully.

    All the same, he must be missing his dad.

    *Mutt growling.*

    [*Looking around*] Mutt? Where are you, boy?

*Mutt scampers over, panting in excitement.* YONG *crouches down to pat the dog but is suddenly bowled over by a looming shadowy figure.*

GEORGE: [*waving a bottle*] Get away! Get away! Don't. Touch. Dog. All of you Chinese, keep away. You think I'm gonna let you lot boil him up with your rice? Not on yer life, you hear me? NOT ON YER LIFE!

*Screeching sound into ...*

*FLASHFORWARD BEGINS.*

*Strobe lighting.*

GEORGE'*s bottle morphs into a rifle. He brandishes it wildly. Mutt barks. The cock of the rifle.* YONG'*s distorted yell. A crack and thud.*

GEORGE *crumples.*

*FLASHFORWARD ENDS.*

## SCENE NINE

*A grey mist.*

YONG *emerges out of the tent, cautious.*

*We hear a kookaburra laugh.*

YONG *turns towards the sound.*

GEORGE: 'Kookaburra! That bird is called a kookaburra!'
YONG: Mr George's gold tooth is glinting in the sun.
    He certainly wasn't smiling last night.
    I want to say to Father, 'This Mr George, he's not a nice man. He's not a good man. I don't think we should follow him to the goldfields.'
    But the words stick in my throat.

GEORGE *imitates the kookaburra's maniacal laugh.*

GEORGE: 'Great sense of humour, innit. Always got something to laugh about. What about you, Chinaboy? Got something funny to share?'
YONG: [*tries to laugh weakly along*] I want to ask him, 'Why do you look at my people like you're better than us?' But I've promised Father.
    I promised to pretend I can't speak English.

To pretend I don't have the words to say what's in my heart,
So others can keep their face.
NING: [*with a clap of his hands*] Yong, Feng, Chung ... Let's march on!

*YONG and others begin to chant, but* YONG *secretly begins to practise his English again.*

YONG: Cloud. Tree. Grass. Mist. Cold.

*They arrive at a well.*

GEORGE: Alright you lot, hurry up and fill up your water containers! We ain't got long.

YONG: This is a Chinese well!

*He runs around, inspecting it.*

They're round like the ones at home; no corners for evil spirits to hide in.

I wonder how long it took to build this?

YONG *sees something shining in the ground. He picks up a necklace with round Chinese coins.*

There would've been many coins on this necklace once.
But I guess the coins hold no value here anymore.

*He looks at the ground and discovers other items.*

Ma used to say it was terrible to leave things behind just because they become a burden in a new place. What would she say about Father selling her sash, leaving it behind in a foreign land?

*Night. The men are gathered around a campfire. Distant sound of dog barking.*

NING: You men think digging for gold will be just like the way we dig our land? No. There's a lot we must learn.

YONG: No-one in the village has even seen gold before.
And Mr Feng's not so sure.

FENG: We need enough gold to take home to our families as well as pay back the moneylenders that got us here. Look how many of us there are! That's a lot of gold to go around.

NING: Foreigners work fast. Too fast. They often leave small gold pickings behind. We can collect what's been overlooked.

*Dog barks excitedly.*

What are you doing, Yong?

*Beat.*

Let Mr George feed his own animal! What are you thinking? *We have miles to go and you are giving our food to feed a dog*? Do you want us to starve?

*Beat.*

Then what, Yong? Explain yourself. Why would you do something so stupid?

YONG: 'Don't call me stupid! You're stupid, dragging the entire village away from their families to this country in the middle of nowhere, looking for gold that might not even exist! And worst of all, Father, I know what you are … you're a thief for stealing something that was mine!'

*Looks at audience.*

That's not what I actually say, of course.

'Sorry, Father. I guess I wasn't thinking.'

I notice beads of sweat on Father's brow even though it's a cool night.

Mr Chung puts out a steady hand.

CHUNG: Yong, you should get to bed. It's late.

YONG: As I walk away, I hear the villagers ask Father,

'Are you alright, Ning?

Don't mind him, he's just a boy, Ning.'

And Father brushing it off with a chuckle.

Father cares so much about saving *his* face, but what about mine?

*Low screeching sound ebbs and flows.*

## SCENE TEN

*Morning.*

*The journey continues.*

YONG: Tree. Grass. Sky. Goldfields.
>Bitter eucalyptus. Jumping kangaroos. Silvery moon.
>Mr George told us to go back to *flowery land* the other day.
>It didn't sound like a compliment.
>*Beat.*

What? We're stopping again?
>*A clanking sound and the whip of another bullocky.*

I look to Father but he puts down his pole, turns and walks down the line to speak to the others. I've never seen him move so stiff and slow.
>YONG *makes his way to the other side of the cart to eavesdrop.*

Mr George is talking to another guide.

GEORGE: Hey there Will.
>Not much rain. More of a drought.
>Big load.
>That's right, [*laughing*] I got me a yellow load!
>Nah. Won't take 'em all the way. Ching Chongs make trouble for everyone.
>How many bottles for this?
>*Clanking sounds of utensils and bottles.*

I'd call that a fair trade.
>Don't worry. I won't take them all the way. I'll know when to stop.
>*Horse hooves departing. Sounds of the chant pick up once more.*

YONG: Won't take *who* all the way *where*?
>Mr George could only have been talking about us.
>But why?
>Why wouldn't he take us all the way to the goldfields?

*Image of dozens of men in grey/blue tunics and conical bamboo hats tilling and hoeing the soil in long, straight rows.*

*Voices of villagers exclaiming in excitement.*

Over there, in the fields!
Just like at home.
The same hats,
The same tunics,
The same pants.
They're Chinese, and they're growing vegetables!
Finally, Father is smiling.

NING: Mr George! We stop! We buy from men.

GEORGE: Oh, so *now* we stop. Alright, fine. Over there is Penola. Once you're done with your vegetables, we'll set up camp outside town.

NING: We'll eat well tonight, Yong. Onions and vegetables from the Chinese growers, and still some money left for rice from the shop tomorrow.

YONG: Father puts his hand on my shoulder.
His face is shiny with sweat.
And the shadows under his eyes are dark.
But I don't want to break this precious moment with him.
Because I don't know when it will happen again.

YONG *smiles at* NING.

Yes, Father.

## SCENE ELEVEN

*Darkness.*

*Dream sequence. Two kites soaring in the sky. We should be able to decipher the blue and silver one as* YONG*'s.*

*The two kites spin towards each other.* NING*'s kite is soaring high, and* YONG *struggles to keep up, beginning to flail.*

*Sound of* NING *groaning in pain.*

YONG *wakes and places a hand on his father's forehead. It is very hot. He places a cool cloth on his father's forehead and goes back to sleep.*

*Morning.*

NING: [*snatching the cloth from his forehead*] Yong, was this you? Why? I'm fine. Come on, hurry up! We have a lot to do today.

> *Sounds of Penola town: horse hooves and carts.*

What's the matter with you, Yong? Your face is like a dried plum.

> *Beat.*

Look, I shouldn't have yelled this morning … I don't want you to worry. I'm as fit as an ox. Look at us. Chung had a fever in Robe Town, Feng gets headaches and I had cramps last night …

YONG: And a fever—

NING: Shush, Yong.

## SCENE TWELVE

*Nightfall.*

YONG: That night
>   We eat like emperors.
>   I can't remember the last time I had rice and fresh vegetables.
>   But Father doesn't have an appetite.
>   I stare hungrily at his bowl while he picks slowly through his meal.
>   Father heads off early again to bed,
>   Mr Chung sits beside me.

His empty socket is no longer a distraction,
It gives focus to his single-eyed gaze.

CHUNG: 'You're only thirteen, but you're keeping up with all of us. Your father must be proud.'

YONG: I wish I could believe him.

Mr George's fire has a wisp of smoke meandering up to the clouded sky.

Perhaps our guide has fallen asleep?

YONG *tiptoes towards Mutt. He grins as the dog sees him.*

[*Whispering*] It's okay, Mutt. It's just me.

YONG *takes another step.*

*Twig snaps. Mutt starts yapping. A shot of the rifle into the air.*

GEORGE: [*slurring, waving his rifle wildly*] Who's there?
Shut up, Mutt!
You!

GEORGE *grabs* YONG *by the arm.*

After my dog again, eh?

*The pounding of feet and cries of the villagers in Chinese.*

*The light of a lantern bounces.*

YONG *is pushed to the ground and staggers to his feet.*

NING: Stop! Leave my son alone, George.
Yong, come here.
You are our guide, George. We have given you money to take us to the goldfields. Nothing more, nothing less. Please remember that.

*Beat.*

Also, there are many more of us than there are of you.

GEORGE: [*snarling*] Are you threatening me, Ning?

NING: Do not try to harm my son again, George.

SCENE THIRTEEN

*The chant, much more subdued than before.*

YONG: The track goes on and on.
　　　　Hardly slept last night.
　　　　Father's fever was up again and now
　　　　His pigtail hardly moves as we trudge along.
　　　　Left and right. Left and right.
　　　　The men were talking about weapons this morning,
　　　　Counting the guns and knives among us.
　　　　'Be alert for accidents!' Father said.
　　　　But the men knew what he really meant.
NING: What is it, Yong?
YONG: It's Mr George, Father.

　　　　*Pause.*

　　I … I heard some words between him and another guide. I think the guide told Mr George not to take us all the way to the goldfields.

　　　　*Beat.*

　　Because there was trouble. Fighting. And that we, Chinese, were to blame.
NING: How can you be sure?
YONG: I don't know. It was the way they spoke—
NING: Yong, haven't you caused enough trouble between us and Mr George? All for the sake of a stupid dog. Do you understand how much danger you've put us all in?

　　　　NING *takes a raspy breath, struggles through the below.*

　　You are only learning English …
YONG: [*as* NING *collapses*] Father!!!
　　　　Help! Please, someone help us!

　　　　*Horses whinny.*

GEORGE: What's wrong with you, Ning?
　　　　Let's go!

　　　　*Peering into his face.*

Jeez, you're real crook, aren't you?
What's the matter, cat got your tongue?
You don't understand? Of course you don't understand, Chinaman.
None of you Chinese understand. That's the problem, innit.
You don't understand that this is our land. Our gold.
We worked bloody hard to build this country and ...
We don't want you here!
What's that? You want to ride in the back of the cart?
Ha! No chance.
I guide you! Not carry you!
And you should've thought of that before you threatened me last night.
How dare you?
You are nothing on this land, do you understand?
You should be grateful we let you in at all.
You walk. Crawl if you have to.
I'm not doing any favours for you lot.
No way.

*Lighting change.*

*The villagers find a campsite for the night.*

CHUNG: Your father's badly dehydrated. We'll need water before dark. Apparently there's a waterhole towards the end of that track, we'll get Feng to ...

YONG: I'll go, Mr Chung. I want to get water for my father.

## SCENE FOURTEEN

*The camp recedes.*

*Clouds cover the sky as* YONG *becomes progressively lost.*

YONG: I walk through the bush. The birds and animals call out; they're saying goodnight to each other, I think. I can hear my heart beating and my blood rushing. Where is this waterhole?

*Singing and the sound of clapsticks.*

Singing? People singing. No, one man singing. I follow the sound; my heart is roaring. I see a man clapping sticks and singing. It's like he's praying, beside him is a boy, like me, except black.

He is crying, tears falling down his face. It looks like a grave, a large one, maybe many people are there.

The boy sees me. I want to run, but he smiles gently at me. I wave before I can stop myself.

He touches the man; I think it's his father. The singing stops and the bush all goes quiet and one bird calls out, a crow. The man turns and sees me. I stand and my legs are shaking.

Please don't hurt me, I'm thinking.

He looks at me and then the grave and then the boy. He sees my empty waterbag. He points down the path past the clearing and I realise he is saying something.

'Parreetch. Parreetch.' (*Water.*)

I walk past but the boy steps toward me and reaches out his hand. We touch, and I keep walking towards the waterhole.

*Repeat of the earlier kite-flying dream sequence. This time,* NING *speaks.*

NING: [*voiceover*] Do not pull the string so hard, Yong. Let yourself be guided by the wind.

*The two kites spin towards each other.* NING*'s kite is soaring high, and* YONG *struggles to keep up, beginning to flail. A gust of wind sends* YONG*'s kite into some branches.* YONG *pulls at it frantically.*

Yong, stay calm. You need to focus and—

*The kite string severs.*

YONG: [*watching his kite float away*] Oh no! … No! No! Noooo …

*His moans fade to be replaced by another's, waking him up from his dream.*

NING: No … No … No …

YONG: Father? Father! It's alright. It's me. Yong. I'm here, Father.

*A lantern beams into the tent. Voices outside.*

Father is burning up. Please get some more water for him!

Let me help with your tunic.

*As the tunic is raised over* NING*'s head,* YONG *sinks onto his knees and sobs with relief. When he lifts his head again, he is* *holding Mother's sash with blue and silver chrysanthemums. He lifts the cloth to his face.*

YONG *folds the sash and places it carefully inside his basket.*

*Then he takes* NING*'s hand.*

YONG: I was wrong about you, Father. You didn't sell Mother's sash.

NING: [*fumbling*] Mei-ling's sash!

YONG: I have it, it's safe.

NING: She loved that sash.

YONG: It was mine, Father. She gave it to me. You had no right to take it.

NING: Are you disrespecting … ?

NING *shuts his eyes, comes to a decision.*

I should not have taken it. It was yours. Your mother … she loved you … but we thought differently.

I thought you must be tougher to become a man. But perhaps you are tough in ways I do not understand …

YONG: [*feeling his forehead*] Father, your fever has gone. We will keep going all the way to the goldfields. And once we've found gold, we'll go home and help our family and visit Ma's grave.

NING: You are a good son, Yong.

YONG: Imagine Grandma's face when we come home with all that gold … Her eyes will crinkle up and she will brag to everyone, 'My son did this! My grandson did this … '

YONG *gradually falls asleep resting his head against* NING*'s chest during the above.*

*Lighting change from night to dawn.*

YONG *wakes up.*

*He realises his father is gone and begins shaking with grief.*

*Wern Mak as Yong in Monkey Baa's production of YONG 2022 (Photo: Tiffany Garvie)*

## SCENE FIFTEEN

*In front of a grave with a stone.*
*Wind. Mutt barks in the distance. The sound of spades digging.*

YONG: For the first time in our journey we are digging.
    But it is not for gold.

> *With a small pebble,* YONG *scratches* '爸爸', *the Chinese characters for 'father', on the stone.*
>
> YONG *takes his mother's sash from his basket and winds it around his waist.*

We bury Father on a small hill facing the ocean.
    I'm told it is the right balance of wind and water.
    And his spirit will ride home on the wings of a crane.

> YONG *bows in respect.*

I will return, Father. Take you back to China and place you next to Ma. I will make you proud.
    I take my place—
    My father's place—
    At the front of the line.
    My legs feel rooted to the spot.
    I cannot move.
    But the other men are waiting.
    They need to move forward.
    Even if it means leaving my father behind.

CHUNG: It's okay, Yong. One step after another. That's all.

> YONG *begins to walk. Behind him, the chant slowly picks up once more.*
>
> *Horses whinny.*

GEORGE: We go! [*Sardonic*] The Headman's son, eh? Or should I say, *Mister* Yong.

> *He laughs.*

Gee-yup!

> *Crack of the whip.*

## SCENE SIXTEEN

*Dark skies.*

*Rainfall. Mutt barking. Sounds of the chant. A river.*
GEORGE *looks upstream, then downstream.*

GEORGE: No! The river's too high to cross.
> *He raises his hand to show the river's too high to cross.*
> *Horse's neigh. They begin to walk again.*

FENG: Come on, Yong!
> A young boy like you should be able to walk faster. Mud or no mud!

YONG: Would your son be able to walk faster than this, Mr Feng?

FENG: Of course. But I wasn't allowed to bring him, was I?

YONG: I came to help my father.
> Perhaps if you also spoke the foreigners' tongue, you could've been the Headman and your son could've come.

FENG: [*surprised but having nothing to say*] Hmmph.
> *A bridge.*
> YONG *and others cross the bridge, battered by wind and rain.*
> *We hear a muffled cry.*

YONG: Mr Li!
> He drops his bamboo pole.
> And stumbles over one of his baskets.
> Toppling towards the edge of the bridge.
> Sliding towards the gushing water underneath.
> 'Mr Li! Hold this!'
> Mr Li's hands fumble, but eventually he grips the pole.
> And we pull him back to centre, back to upright.

GEORGE: Hurry up, you lot! We haven't got all day!

YONG: Every fibre of my being wants to scream at Mr George to stop.
> To acknowledge that one of us is injured.
> To treat us like humans
> Instead of animals less worthy than his dog.
> But how to do that *and* keep my promise to my father?

*Beat.*
We continue.

## SCENE SEVENTEEN

*The chant, more fatigued than ever.*
*YONG is trudging wearily.*
*A bird flashes past with bright red wings. Or is it a kite? In YONG's confusion, he reaches up as if to catch it.*
*FLASHFORWARD BEGINS.*
*Strobe lighting.*
*A severed pigtail is swung triumphantly in the air.* CHUNG's *hand reaches up to the back of a scalp and is smeared with blood.*
*The actor performs traces of the Flashforward movement motif.*
*Mutt barks. The cock of the rifle. Crack. Thud.*
*FLASHFORWARD ENDS.*
YONG *faints.*
*We hear Mother's voice singing to* YONG *as a child.*

## SCENE EIGHTEEN

CHUNG: Stay there, Yong.
    You've had a fall.
    How do you feel?
YONG: Strange. How long have I been here, Mr Chung?
CHUNG: Only ten minutes.
   *Pause.*
  Do you want to keep walking?
YONG: What do you mean?
  [*Biting his lip*] I would like to go home and fly my kite.
CHUNG: [*smiling*] Ahhh, kites.
   *Beat.*
  It is not impossible to get you home if that's what you really want.

YONG: Would you go home if you were me?
CHUNG: If I had family to go home to, probably. But the war... I have no-one now.
> *Pause.*

YONG: Did you have a son, Mr Chung?
CHUNG: Yes. I was a father once.
> But the past is the past.
> *The howling of the wind.*

YONG: But the past is never truly gone, is it?
> It is still here, as if we can touch it.
> It continues to live through us in the present moment.
> *YONG stands and shakes out the cloth and picks up his belongings.*
>
> I'd like to keep walking, Mr Chung.

## SCENE NINETEEN

*Clink-clank sound of another cart approaching.*

GEORGE: [*raising his hand*] Hoy! Are you looking to trade, mate? I'll be needing some refreshments.
> How many bottles for this one?
> Nah, they won't be needing it, are you kidding?
> I won't be taking them all the way ... if you get me.
> *Sound of equipment being exchanged for bottles of booze.*

Good doing business with you.
> Gee-yup!
> *Lighting change focus to* YONG*'s face, who's heard and understood everything.*

CHUNG: Yong, are you okay? You look like you've seen a ghost.
YONG: I feel like I *have* seen a ghost, Mr Chung.
> My father's ghost.
> I made him a promise that I think I have to break.
> Otherwise I'm afraid a lot of people will get hurt.
> *Beat.*

Mr George has been stealing from us. He's been trading our mining equipment for drink, and he's not planning to take us to the goldfields after all.

*Pause.*

Father taught me English. But he made me keep it secret so that no-one would lose face. I made this promise to him, but now I've broken it.

YONG *begins to weep from both shame and relief.*

CHUNG: Your father would understand, Yong. Let's go find this Mr George.

## SCENE TWENTY

*Sound of crackling fires and night noises.*

GEORGE *muttering/singing drunkenly to himself.*

GEORGE: See my gun, Mutt? Bang! Bang! No more Chinese! Just like that. Bang! Bang!

*Leaves and twigs crunching underfoot.*

Who's that?

*He sees* CHUNG *and* YONG.

Get away, both of you! Stay away from my dog! I see you, you little thief!

YONG: [*in English*] No. You are the thief, Mr George. Not me. You take things from cart. You talk to other guides, I hear. You speak to Mutt, I hear!

GEORGE: [*stunned*] Liar!

*Voices of the villagers as they start to gather around the ruckus.*

YONG: I know English. You tell Mutt, you want to shoot us!

I see the glint of a knife … Mr Chung!

GEORGE: You long-haired devil!

GEORGE *hurls himself at* CHUNG *and kicks* CHUNG *to the ground.*

GEORGE *swoops down with a knife, and with a loud grunt, hacks at the back of* CHUNG*'s head. In a flash, he holds up and swings his pigtail like a dead animal.*

CHUNG *struggles to his feet, holding the back of his scalp, revealing a hand covered in blood.*

YONG: Mr George grabs his rifle.

GEORGE: Tell them I want everything they own in this cart. Now!

YONG: Everybody, stay calm. Put your belongings in Mr George's cart.

*A confusion of sounds:* GEORGE's *shouts, the clanking of equipment, the fear of the villagers.*

YONG *grabs a thick branch nearby and drops to the ground. He wriggles around the back of the cart and clambers up. He lifts the branch up just as—*

*Mutt barks. The cock of the rifle. Crack. Thud.*

## SCENE TWENTY-ONE

*Dawn.*

YONG *touches the sash around his middle.*

FENG: [*calling out*] You know that many words, Yong? Enough to understand that Mr George was scheming against us all this time?

YONG: Yes, Mr Feng. I do.

YONG *walks to* GEORGE, *who is roped up by the cart.*

Mr George, we will make our own way to the goldfields, but we will need the cart for our belongings. We will leave you food and water, and let others know where to find and untie you.

GEORGE: Take the dog.

*Beat.*

[*Snarling*] Take the dog! I'm not sharing my food with him. Take Mutt!

YONG: Come on, Mutt!

*Mutt yaps happily.*

Good boy, Mutt.

[*To* GEORGE] You have caused a lot of harm, Mr George. I hope we never meet anyone like you again in Australia.

YONG *lifts his wares. Seeing* CHUNG, *he bows.*

Mr Chung's head is still in bandages.
He avoided me last night.
He avoided everyone.
He feels he's lost face.
Because having your pigtail cut off by a foreigner
Is supposed to be a terrible humiliation.

CHUNG: You saved my life yesterday, Yong, I am deeply indebted to you. We all are.

CHUNG *reaches to touch the back of his head where his pigtail was and hunches in shame.*

YONG: Mr Chung, will you drive the cart for us to the goldfields?

CHUNG: I don't think I'm the right person, Yong. Not … now.

YONG: [*blurting*] You haven't lost face in my eyes, Mr Chung. You are a man of courage and what happened to your hair doesn't change that. If you don't guide the horses to Ballarat and someone like Mr Feng does it instead, we might end up back in Robe Town!

CHUNG *laughs in surprise.*

CHUNG: Alright, Yong. I will do it for you.

YONG *smiles and claps his hands together.*

*Mutt barks.*

YONG: Let's march on.

*Chanting begins.*

## SCENE TWENTY-TWO

*A deep fog lifts to reveal a sign with carved Chinese characters and an arrow.*

YONG: Ballarat!

>*A bird calls.*

>Father, I made it.
>>I finished the journey you started.
>>I finished the journey you wanted;
>>I made it mine.
>>I have walked.
>>I have broken a promise.
>>And I have arrived.

CHUNG: Here, Yong, I have something for you. Close your eyes. Now open them.

>*YONG opens his eyes and sees in his hands a kite made from four firm twigs and old tent scraps. He grins.*

YONG: See that, Ma? There's just enough wind for it today.

>*YONG begins to run, lifting the kite up behind him.*

>*The kite dances up towards the clouds, floating above the goldfields.*

THE END

# More plays for young audiences from Currency Press

PETE THE SHEEP, THE PLAY

*Adapted for the stage by Eva Di Cesare, Tim McGarry and Sandra Eldridge. Music by Phillip Scott*

*Based on the picture book by Jackie French and Bruce Whatley*

Shaun the Shearer just wants to give smokin' haircuts to sheep. Unfortunately the other shearers on the station don't like Shaun's new-fangled ways – he even has a sheep-sheep instead of a sheepdog! Shaun and his partner Pete the Sheep set up their own creative hair salon in town. Before long word is out and all the sheep in town are down for a do, and maybe even the big boys too! Pete the Sheep is a lively and mischievous award-winning musical about individual expression, for young and old.

ISBN: 9781925005431

# HITLER'S DAUGHTER

*Adapted by Eva Di Cesare, Sandra Eldridge and Tim McGarry from the novel by Jackie French*

Did Hitler really have a daughter? And if he did, what happened to her? As four children wait for the school bus on a rainy morning in the Australian countryside, they take it in turns to tell stories. On this particular morning, Anna tells a story about a young girl, Heidi, whose father was one of the most notorious men of the twentieth century. As the play jumps between Germany in the 1940s and the Australian bush in the present day, each of the characters is confronted with issues of morality, personal responsibility and humanity. Adapted from the prize-winning novel, Hitler's Daughter is a tautly written tale of suspense with a deeply human heart.

ISBN: 9780868198132

# THURSDAY'S CHILD

*Adapted by Eva Di Cesare, Sandra Eldridge and Tim McGarry from the novel by Sonya Hartnett*

Tin Flute was born on a Thursday. He is a reclusive child who is more at home in the subterranean tunnels he digs under his family's farm than he is above ground. As his impoverished family struggles for survival in rural Australia during the Great Depression, Tin retreats further underground into a world of darkness and troubling secrets. Adapted from Sonya Hartnett's novel, Thursday's Child is a surreal and epic piece of theatre that explores the themes of memory, fate, family camaraderie and the spirit of determination when faced with cruel misfortune. Teacher's notes are available.

ISBN: 9780868198873

BOY OVERBOARD

*Adapted by Patricia Cornelius from the novel by Morris Gleitzman*

Jamal and Bibi have a dream: to lead Australia to soccer glory in the next World Cup… but first they must face landmines, pirates, storms and a sinking ship. Can Jamal and his family survive their incredible journey and get to Australia? Boy Overboard depicts a deeply human side of the asylum seeker issue by following the journey of Jamal and Bibi from Afghanistan to Australia. Inspired by real life events, this is a moving and often funny play about young people overcoming the confusion of war and politics in search of their safe haven.

ISBN: 9780868198071

# HONEY SPOT
*Jack Davis*

One of Jack Davis' most celebrated theatrical works, Honey Spot is a play about friendship and its power to bring worlds and cultures together. A young girl makes friends with the new boy at school. Peggy is a budding dancer and daughter of the local forest ranger, Tim lives in a forestry-owned house and dances to the rhythm of his cousin's didgeridoo. As their friendship grows, Tim agrees to help Peggy create a dance piece for the ballet scholarship competition – and together, they blend the earthy feel of traditional Noongar dance and the fluid grace of classical ballet into one. First staged in Western Australia in 1985 during the emerging reconciliation movement, Honey Spot is an optimistic, funny and moving story about the power of friendship to overcome racial differences and prejudices.

ISBN: 9780868191638

# MASQUERADE

*Kate Mulvany, based on the book by Kit Williams*

In a wondrous world of riddles and hidden treasure, bumbling Jack Hare is on a race against time to deliver a message of love from the Moon to the Sun. Far, far away in a world just like ours, a mother cheers her son Joe with the tale of Jack Hare's adventure. But when Jack's mission goes topsy-turvy, Joe and his mum must come to the rescue, and the line between the two worlds becomes blurred forever. Bringing to life Kit Williams' iconic picture book, Masquerade stars a talking fish, a tone-deaf barbershop quartet, a gassy pig, a precious jewel and a few mere mortals. It's a magical adventure that is, at its heart, about the love between a parent and a child.

ISBN: 9781925005844

## www.currency.com.au

Visit Currency Press' website now to:

- Order books
- Browse through our full list of titles including plays, screenplays, theory and reference/criticism, performance handbooks, educational texts and more
- Choose a play for your school or performance group by cast specs
- Seek performance rights
- Find out about performing arts news and sign up for our newsletter
- For students: read our study guides
- For teachers: access free curriculum information and teacher notes

We are also on Facebook and Instagram (@currencypress). Join the conversation!

### The performing arts publisher

www.ingramcontent.com/pod-product-compliance
Lightning Source LLC
Chambersburg PA
CBHW050027090426
42734CB00021B/3453